Gymnastics Journal

This Journal Belongs To:

_____

Copyright © 2017 CastleGate Designs

CastleGate Sports Journals

All rights reserved. No part of this book may be reproduced or redistributed without express permission from the author and publishing company.

Graphics courtesy of Vecteezy.com and Getty Images. Any graphic images are used with permission and the appropriate commercial use licenses.

ISBN-10: 1981281908
ISBN-13: 978-1981281909

Dedication

This journal is dedicated to every girl and boy, man and woman who share a passion for the sport and art of gymnastics. May this journal help you achieve all your gymnastics goals.

Table of Contents

Welcome	page 7
Gymnastics Goals	page 9
Testing Records	page 15
Competitions	page 21
Practice Notes	page 29

Welcome to the Gymnastics Journal. This journal will help you to record all your testing accomplishments, competition results, and notes from your practices. It is meant to help you organize your goals, keep track of your progress, and have a record of your journey in the fantastic sport of gymnastics!

In the Goals section, write down the goals that you have for your gymnastics progress. Include the date that you made the goal, the date you want to have it completed, and the steps you plan to take to achieve that goal.

In the Testing section, record of all the tests you have attempted. Record the name of the test, date, place, result of the test, and any notes you want to remember about the test.

In the Competition section, record all the competitions you participate in. Include the name of the competition and where it was held, the date, your event name, your result (for example, 1st out of 10), the music that you performed to if applicable, and any notes you want to remember about the competition.

In the Practice Notes section, record notes from your practices with your coaches. Include the date, gym, the name of the coach, what skills you worked on, and what things you want to remember from the practice, like tips from your coach or things that worked for a skill. Keeping notes on your practices will be a tremendous help for progressing quickly in your journey to be a great gymnast.

GYMNASTICS GOALS

Gymnastics Goals

Gymnastics Goal	Date Made	Goal Date	Steps to Achieve Goal	Done

Gymnastics Goals

Gymnastics Goal	Date Made	Goal Date	Steps to Achieve Goal	Done

Gymnastics Goals

Gymnastics Goal	Date Made	Goal Date	Steps to Achieve Goal	Done

Gymnastics Goals

Gymnastics Goal	Date Made	Goal Date	Steps to Achieve Goal	Done

TESTING RECORDS

Testing

Test Name	Date	Place	Result	Notes

TESTING

Test Name	Date	Place	Result	Notes

Testing

Test Name	Date	Place	Result	Notes

Testing

Test Name	Date	Place	Result	Notes

Gymnastics Competitions

Competitions

Competition Name	Date	Event	Result	Music	Notes

Competitions

Competition Name	Date	Event	Result	Music	Notes

Competitions

Competition Name	Date	Event	Result	Music	Notes

Competitions

Competition Name	Date	Event	Result	Music	Notes

Competitions

Competition Name	Date	Event	Result	Music	Notes

Competitions

Competition Name	Date	Event	Result	Music	Notes

Practice Notes

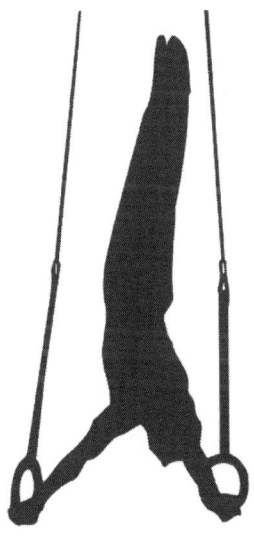

Practice Notes

Practice Date	Place	Coach
Skills Practiced	**Things to Remember**	

Practice Date	Place	Coach
Skills Practiced	**Things to Remember**	

Practice Notes

Practice Date	Place	Coach
Skills Practiced	Things to Remember	

Practice Date	Place	Coach
Skills Practiced	Things to Remember	

Practice Notes

Practice Date	Place	Coach
Skills Practiced	Things to Remember	

Practice Date	Place	Coach
Skills Practiced	Things to Remember	

Practice Notes

Practice Date	Place	Coach
Skills Practiced	Things to Remember	

Practice Date	Place	Coach
Skills Practiced	Things to Remember	

Practice Notes

Practice Date	Place	Coach
Skills Practiced	Things to Remember	

Practice Date	Place	Coach
Skills Practiced	Things to Remember	

Practice Notes

Practice Date	Place	Coach
Skills Practiced	**Things to Remember**	

Practice Date	Place	Coach
Skills Practiced	**Things to Remember**	

Practice Notes

Practice Date	Place	Coach
Skills Practiced	Things to Remember	

Practice Date	Place	Coach
Skills Practiced	Things to Remember	

Practice Notes

Practice Date	Place	Coach
Skills Practiced	Things to Remember	

Practice Date	Place	Coach
Skills Practiced	Things to Remember	

Practice Notes

Practice Date	Place	Coach
Skills Practiced	**Things to Remember**	

Practice Date	Place	Coach
Skills Practiced	**Things to Remember**	

Practice Notes

Practice Date	Place	Coach
Skills Practiced	**Things to Remember**	

Practice Date	Place	Coach
Skills Practiced	**Things to Remember**	

Practice Notes

Practice Date	Place	Coach
Skills Practiced	Things to Remember	

Practice Date	Place	Coach
Skills Practiced	Things to Remember	

Practice Notes

Practice Date	Place	Coach
Skills Practiced	Things to Remember	

Practice Date	Place	Coach
Skills Practiced	Things to Remember	

Practice Notes

Practice Date	Place	Coach
Skills Practiced	Things to Remember	

Practice Date	Place	Coach
Skills Practiced	Things to Remember	

Practice Notes

Practice Date	Place	Coach
Skills Practiced	Things to Remember	

Practice Date	Place	Coach
Skills Practiced	Things to Remember	

Practice Notes

Practice Date	Place	Coach
Skills Practiced	**Things to Remember**	

Practice Date	Place	Coach
Skills Practiced	**Things to Remember**	

Practice Notes

Practice Date	Place	Coach
Skills Practiced	**Things to Remember**	

Practice Date	Place	Coach
Skills Practiced	**Things to Remember**	

Practice Notes

Practice Date	Place	Coach
Skills Practiced	Things to Remember	

Practice Date	Place	Coach
Skills Practiced	Things to Remember	

Practice Notes

Practice Date	Place	Coach
Skills Practiced	Things to Remember	

Practice Date	Place	Coach
Skills Practiced	Things to Remember	

Practice Notes

Practice Date	Place	Coach
Skills Practiced	**Things to Remember**	

Practice Date	Place	Coach
Skills Practiced	**Things to Remember**	

Practice Notes

Practice Date	Place	Coach
Skills Practiced	Things to Remember	

Practice Date	Place	Coach
Skills Practiced	Things to Remember	

Practice Notes

Practice Date	Place	Coach
Skills Practiced	**Things to Remember**	

Practice Date	Place	Coach
Skills Practiced	**Things to Remember**	

Practice Notes

Practice Date	Place	Coach
Skills Practiced	Things to Remember	

Practice Date	Place	Coach
Skills Practiced	Things to Remember	

Practice Notes

Practice Date	Place	Coach
Skills Practiced	Things to Remember	

Practice Date	Place	Coach
Skills Practiced	Things to Remember	

Practice Notes

Practice Date	Place	Coach
Skills Practiced	Things to Remember	

Practice Date	Place	Coach
Skills Practiced	Things to Remember	

Practice Notes

Practice Date	Place	Coach
Skills Practiced	Things to Remember	

Practice Date	Place	Coach
Skills Practiced	Things to Remember	

Practice Notes

Practice Date	Place	Coach
Skills Practiced	**Things to Remember**	

Practice Date	Place	Coach
Skills Practiced	**Things to Remember**	

Practice Notes

Practice Date	Place	Coach
Skills Practiced	Things to Remember	

Practice Date	Place	Coach
Skills Practiced	Things to Remember	

Practice Notes

Practice Date	Place	Coach
Skills Practiced	Things to Remember	

Practice Date	Place	Coach
Skills Practiced	Things to Remember	

Practice Notes

Practice Date	Place	Coach
Skills Practiced	**Things to Remember**	

Practice Date	Place	Coach
Skills Practiced	**Things to Remember**	

Practice Notes

Practice Date	Place	Coach
Skills Practiced	Things to Remember	

Practice Date	Place	Coach
Skills Practiced	Things to Remember	

Practice Notes

Practice Date	Place	Coach
Skills Practiced	Things to Remember	

Practice Date	Place	Coach
Skills Practiced	Things to Remember	

Practice Notes

Practice Date	Place	Coach
Skills Practiced	Things to Remember	

Practice Date	Place	Coach
Skills Practiced	Things to Remember	

Practice Notes

Practice Date	Place	Coach
Skills Practiced	Things to Remember	

Practice Date	Place	Coach
Skills Practiced	Things to Remember	

Practice Notes

Practice Date	Place	Coach
Skills Practiced	**Things to Remember**	

Practice Date	Place	Coach
Skills Practiced	**Things to Remember**	

Practice Notes

Practice Date	Place	Coach
Skills Practiced	Things to Remember	

Practice Date	Place	Coach
Skills Practiced	Things to Remember	

Practice Notes

Practice Date	Place	Coach
Skills Practiced	Things to Remember	

Practice Date	Place	Coach
Skills Practiced	Things to Remember	

Practice Notes

Practice Date	Place	Coach
Skills Practiced	**Things to Remember**	

Practice Date	Place	Coach
Skills Practiced	**Things to Remember**	

Practice Notes

Practice Date	Place	Coach
Skills Practiced	Things to Remember	

Practice Date	Place	Coach
Skills Practiced	Things to Remember	

Practice Notes

Practice Date	Place	Coach
Skills Practiced	Things to Remember	

Practice Date	Place	Coach
Skills Practiced	Things to Remember	

Practice Notes

Practice Date	Place	Coach
Skills Practiced	**Things to Remember**	

Practice Date	Place	Coach
Skills Practiced	**Things to Remember**	

Practice Notes

Practice Date	Place	Coach
Skills Practiced	Things to Remember	

Practice Date	Place	Coach
Skills Practiced	Things to Remember	

Practice Notes

Practice Date	Place	Coach
Skills Practiced	Things to Remember	

Practice Date	Place	Coach
Skills Practiced	Things to Remember	

Practice Notes

Practice Date	Place	Coach
Skills Practiced	Things to Remember	

Practice Date	Place	Coach
Skills Practiced	Things to Remember	

Practice Notes

Practice Date	Place	Coach
Skills Practiced	Things to Remember	

Practice Date	Place	Coach
Skills Practiced	Things to Remember	

Practice Notes

Practice Date	Place	Coach
Skills Practiced	Things to Remember	

Practice Date	Place	Coach
Skills Practiced	Things to Remember	

Practice Notes

Practice Date	Place	Coach
Skills Practiced	Things to Remember	

Practice Date	Place	Coach
Skills Practiced	Things to Remember	

Practice Notes

Practice Date	Place	Coach
Skills Practiced	Things to Remember	

Practice Date	Place	Coach
Skills Practiced	Things to Remember	

Practice Notes

Practice Date	Place	Coach
Skills Practiced	Things to Remember	

Practice Date	Place	Coach
Skills Practiced	Things to Remember	

Practice Notes

Practice Date	Place	Coach
Skills Practiced	Things to Remember	

Practice Date	Place	Coach
Skills Practiced	Things to Remember	

Practice Notes

Practice Date	Place	Coach
Skills Practiced	Things to Remember	

Practice Date	Place	Coach
Skills Practiced	Things to Remember	

Printed in Great Britain
by Amazon